BUSINESS TRUTHS

96 PROVEN WAYS TO BUILD LOYALTY,
GROW PROFITS, AND SUCCEED
AT EVERYTHING IN BETWEEN

ANDREW BROWN, BA, MES
ROBERT GOLD, MBA, FCPA, FCA

2014 Paperback Edition, First Printing

© 2014 by Chartered Professional Accountants Canada

All rights reserved.

No part of this book may be reproduced or transmitted in any form or by any means, electronic or mechanical, including photocopying, recording, or by any information storage and retrieval system, without permission in writing from the authors.

For more information regarding permission to reprint material from the book, please email your request to the authors:
Robert@BusinessCast.ca or Andrew@BusinessCast.ca.

Cover Design by Mike Spencer
Text Design by Mike Spencer

Published by Easy Marketing Now Corp., Toronto, Canada, proprietor of the BusinessCast Podcast

ABOUT THE AUTHORS

Robert Gold, MBA, FCPA, FCA

For over 20 years, Robert Gold has been the managing partner of CPA firm Bennett Gold LLP in Toronto, where he counsels entrepreneurs, startups and business leaders in all aspects of business strategy and effective planning. He has been a guest lecturer at all Toronto-area universities and colleges on the subject of entrepreneurship and e-commerce and speaks to medical professionals advising on the business of being in practice. Robert has co-written three business books and is a member of CPA Canada's Small and Medium-Sized Practices Advisory Group.

Andrew Z. Brown, BA, MES

Andrew Brown has been a leader in B2B marketing strategy and communications for 20 years. He has advised executives and senior management teams in 15 industries – launching over 150 products and services. Andrew has co-written three business books and over 300 articles that have appeared in The Financial Post, The Globe and Mail, Marketing Magazine, Canadian Retailer, DotCommerce, Direct Marketing News, TechVibes, Vue Magazine, the CMA blog, and several other industry association journals.

Together, Robert and Andrew co-host the BusinessCast podcast, Canada's leading podcast for entrepreneurs, business owners and managers. The BusinessCast has a weekly following of thousands of loyal listeners across Canada and the United States.

ACKNOWLEDGMENTS

The authors thank the hundreds of insightful guests of the BusinessCast, each of whom has given the show its depth and breadth, making it Canada's leading podcast for entrepreneurs and business leaders.

Robert thanks Cindy Daly for listening to him ramble on about the BusinessCast and all things podcast. Robert also thanks Stuart, Katie, and Dara for letting him go on-and-on about all things tech and otherwise. Sometimes they listen.

Andrew thanks Shanan for being a source of unwavering support and constant inspiration.

We would like to express our appreciation to Helen Wilkie who helped us capture the essence of our guests' stories and insights.

And to the 100,000+ listeners of the BusinessCast, across North America, we heartily thank you for listening and sharing your genuine feedback.

And finally, to Steve Jobs, for opening iTunes to independent podcasts. That's all it took.

You can easily subscribe to the BusinessCast for free in iTunes at http://bit.ly/SubscribeBusinessCast

Robert Gold and Andrew Z. Brown

FOREWORD BY CHRIS CARDER

Chris Carder, along with David Dougherty and Gary Fung, co-founded Toronto-based innovation firm and incubator Kinetic Cafe

Business Truths...

As leaders and entrepreneurs, our journey to find business truths spurs innovation. It's what helps us to uncover exciting, game-changing ways for tackling real-world problems.

At the same time, business truths provide inspiration. They awake in us deep passions that propel us and our teams, with varying skills and perspectives, to come together to achieve fantastic accomplishments; things that even surprise ourselves.

Finally, business truths are enlightening. They help us to focus our energies and resources on those things that have the greatest impact – even when those truths are at odds with what we may have originally envisioned or wanted.

Business truths are the source of tremendous power.

But as much as they are powerful, business truths are even more elusive. The speed at which change sneaks up on our every day work lives makes it difficult to pin them down. Technologies, demographics, economies and social values are forever shifting. Trends come and go, opportunities emerge and quickly evaporate.

But rather than dissuade us, this reality further fuels our thirst for business truths. And as an active proponent of businesses in Canada, I find that encouraging.

Having built and grown one of Canada's most successful digital marketing companies and co-founded Kinetic Café – an innovation firm and thriving incubator – I've felt the power of business truths. As a result, I've shared with clients the business truths that opened their eyes to possibilities and catapulted them years ahead of their competitors. I have felt the very personal pain caused by those business truths that compelled me to disband exceptional teams. I've also celebrated with founders, senior management, and investors when business truths led to outstanding returns.

That's why I jumped at the chance to introduce "Business Truths: 96 Proven Ways to Build Loyalty, Grow Profits, and Succeed at Everything In Between".

Business truths are at the heart of every BusinessCast podcast episode – the source of the content for "Business Truths". As co-hosts of the BusinessCast, Canada's most successful business podcast, Robert Gold and Andrew Brown are unflinching about revealing business truths, distilling them, and bringing them to business leaders in a fun and captivating way. They have given rise to a new kind of business journalism, one that ignores the hype of the day. Their business telling cuts through all of the noise that is common in today's fast-paced, increasingly complex and multi-channelled world.

At the end of the day, the "Business Truths" that Robert and Andrew highlight will get us through the tough times and propel us forward. They allow us to build and sustain one of the world's most exciting and prosperous economies. By capturing the insights and lessons from many of the greatest business minds in the world today, Robert and Andrew empower every entrepreneur and business leader to be more successful. That is a business truth that is worth sharing.

Chris Carder
Co-Founder, Kinetic Cafe Inc.
@cwcarder and @kineticcafe

CONTENTS

Introduction   i

PART I: BUSINESS TRUTHS TO BUILD LOYALTY

1. **Listening: For Greater Revenues, Outstanding Staff and Staying Ahead of Competitors**   1
   Featuring Mike Pratt, President and CEO, Best Buy Canada

2. **Challenging the Norm to Gain Market Share**   5
   Featuring Peter Aceto, President and CEO, ING Direct Canada

3. **Tapping Into Communities for Awareness and Sales**   9
   Featuring Julie Cole, Co-founder and Vice-President, Mabel's Labels

4. **Using Customer Conferences: The Ultimate Feedback Tool**   14
   Featuring Eran Farajun, VP Business Development, Asigra Inc.

5. **Succeeding in a Crowded Market: Being Unique in Those Things that Matter**   18
   Featuring Aaron Serruya, CEO, Yogurty's, Yogen Fruz, Jamba Juice Canada

6. **Creating Innovative Products**   22
   Featuring Simon Brightman, Co-Founder, AcceleratorU,

Section Summary: Business Truths To Build Loyalty   26

PART II: BUSINESS TRUTHS TO GROW PROFITS

7. **Keeping it Real**   33
   Dani Reiss, President and CEO, Canada Goose

8. **Bootstrapping To Success** — 39
   Featuring Alex Savva, Co-founder, PharmaFreak

9. **Starting Lean, Gathering Momentum — Then Iterating** — 42
   Featuring Derek Szeto, Co-founder, Dossiya

10. **Creating a Great Culture, Great Teams and Great Products** — 45
    Featuring Albert Lai, Co-founder and CEO, Big Viking Games

Section Summary: Business Truths To Grow Profits — 50

PART III: BUSINESS TRUTHS TO SUCCEED AT EVERYTHING IN BETWEEN

11. **Transforming An Industry** — 55
    Featuring Julia Hartz, Co-Founder, Eventbrite

12. **Finding and Keeping the Right Employees** — 60
    Featuring Dave MacDonald, CEO and President, Softchoice

13. **Manufacturing Success: It's All About Control** — 64
    Featuring Claudia Harvey and Wendy Johansson, Co-founders, DigIt Handwear

14. **Renting or Buying Your Business Premises: Making the Right Decision** — 68
    Featuring Dianne Usher, President, Toronto Real Estate Board

15. **Turning Your Brand Into News** — 71
    Featuring Alyssa Lioutas and Jennifer Love, Partners in Duet Public Relations

16. **Building Strategic Alliances That Work** — 75
    Featuring Phil Hogg, President, Association of Strategic Alliance Professionals Toronto

17. Preparing For Exponential Growth   79
     Featuring P. Bruce Hunter, CEO and President of Lighthouse360

18. Leveraging The Power of Video   84
     Featuring Mark Campbell, Account Director, VMG Cinematic

19. What Steve Jobs Would Do   88
     Highlights of author Peter Sander's book What Would Steve Jobs Do?

20. Achieving An Effective Balance   91
     Featuring Arlene Dickinson, CEO, Venture Communications and Founder, You Inc.

Section Summary: Business Truths To Succeed At Everything In Between   95

INTRODUCTION

We heard horror stories…

We have seen first-hand the results of companies adopting the wrong business advice. The rapid spread of digital technologies and social media created exciting business opportunities. But, those same technologies and social networks opened the door for an array of business pundits and so-called experts who were spreading harmful business facts, stories and opinions.

Since business owners and leaders need relevant and practical insights – those which are built upon a foundation of real-world experience – we launched the BusinessCast podcast. Our goal was simple: we wanted to provide listeners with a source of information they could trust, a format that respected their hectic lives, and content that would enable them to achieve their ambitious goals. Since 2007, the BusinessCast has successfully quenched the growing thirst for timely, accurate and powerful business truths.

In writing this book we drew upon our BusinessCast podcast because it serves as the source of inspiration to thousands of business owners and leaders every week.

Our challenge: how to choose from hundreds of interviews with many of North America's most respected business and thought leaders and intrepid entrepreneurs.

We've had in-depth conversations with business superstars – Peter Aceto (President, ING Direct Canada), Brian Church (President, LinkedIn Canada), John Sculley (former President of Apple and Pepsi), Chris O'Neill (Country Director, Google Canada), Arlene Dickinson (best known from Canada's television business pitch show the 'Dragons' Den'), Carl Yankowski (former CEO, Reebok and President of Sony), marketing guru, Seth Godin…and the list goes on. We've spoken to people at all stages of business maturity – from starting up a new business through to expanding international powerhouses. We've covered over 100 different industries and discussed the glamorous, as well as the routine, aspects of business.

Given this wealth of business insight, where should we begin?

The answer came from our growing listening community. Business owners and leaders from across Canada frequently shared with us that the BusinessCast provides them with practical and actionable insights. In their words, we give them business truths that help them measurably improve their companies and ultimately, their lives. Delivering practical business truths was at the heart of why we started the BusinessCast podcast and it continues to be our mantra.

The next challenge was how to transform the business truths captured in the BusinessCast episodes from 15 minutes of intense conversation into short, readable prose. We decided to use each episode as a "stand-alone" workshop which meant we kept our guests' stories and insights intact. Then to make sure that Business Truths was well-founded, practical, and actionable, we reviewed the 300+ podcast episodes and distilled those into 96 business truths within 20 chapters. These truths can be applied across all companies, regardless of size, industry, age, or geographic location.

What emerged were the two priorities that business owners and leaders focus upon every day: building loyalty and growing profits. Of course, the distance between these two "goal posts" can be razor thin or a vast chasm. That "in between" space is the day-to-day "organized chaos" that is involved in building and sustaining a successful business. In other words, it is the messy blending of the full range of business issues.

In the confines of one book, we knew we weren't going to solve every business challenge. But we knew we could chip away at those "keep-you-up-at-night" issues by providing well-founded and practical actions. Thanks to our BusinessCast podcast guests and our community of loyal listeners, Business Truths will help you achieve greatness in building loyalty, growing profits and succeeding at everything in between.

Robert Gold and Andrew Z. Brown
Co-Hosts, The BusinessCast

The BusinessCast is Canada's Top Business Podcast.
You can listen and subscribe to the BusinessCast (for free) in iTunes, or at
http://bit.ly/SubscribeBusinessCast

Robert Gold, MBA, FCPA, FCA
Robert@BusinessCast.ca

Andrew Z. Brown, MES
Andrew@BusinessCast.ca

PART I:

BUSINESS TRUTHS TO BUILD LOYALTY

CHAPTER 1

LISTENING: FOR GREATER REVENUES, OUTSTANDING STAFF AND STAYING AHEAD OF COMPETITORS

Featuring Mike Pratt, President and CEO, Best Buy Canada

The retail landscape is changing rapidly, and Best Buy Canada is one of the players contributing to that change with its ever-evolving business model.

According to President and CEO Mike Pratt, an area of constant challenge is marketing and, specifically, where to spend advertising and marketing budgets. On one side lies traditional marketing such as broadcast television, radio, direct mail and fliers. On the other hand there is digital advertising and social platforms such as Facebook, LinkedIn, Twitter and Pinterest. Finding the right mix, and the right level of involvement with each, is the challenge Pratt tackles every day.

Listening to Customers

Today's customers want to participate with the retailers they buy from and social platforms make this convenient and easy. So savvy retailers like Best Buy know that if they want to get their message out to customers, they have to be there too. But what should they do there?

People don't just want to listen and receive information or marketing messages — they want to get their two cents' worth in.

The answer rests in recognizing that customers – particularly advocates and detractors – regularly talk about products and services using social media channels. Since they are sharing with the world what they think of companies and their products, it's vital that companies "actively listen" to customers to learn what they want, when they want it, and the kind of experience they demand.

According to Mike Pratt, one message that comes across loud and clear is that customers want: 1) relevant product choices; 2) fast and competent service; and 3) outstanding retail experiences – online and in-store. Best Buy is spending its energies on integrating its web offerings with its stores to give customers this winning combination.

Listening to Employees

One of the foundations for effectively delivering the winning combination to clients is by staffing operations well. To that end, Best Buy has effectively extended its "listening" strategy into their Human Resources strategy to address the perpetual challenge of finding, keeping and rewarding strong performers. As a result, the retailer is constantly creating diverse benefit packages to meet the specific and divergent needs of its current and would-be employees. And these are not run-of-the-mill benefits. For example, the military reservist-leave policy allows employees to serve in the forces while still employed at Best Buy. All employees can also use any type of device they want at work as a much-desired "perk". Furthermore, Best Buy has implemented a "Results Oriented Work Environment" which gives some employees the flexibility to work from home on flexible hours, as long as they achieve the expected results.

Listening often and listening well isn't limited to Best Buy's Human Resources, Customer Support or Marketing functions. Pratt himself uses his own Twitter account to engage with employees and customers alike. He also does a series of videos (telly.com/bbycpresident), in which he directly answers individual customers' questions and concerns.

Listening to Competitors

While other retailers may feel intimidated by having to face competitors like retail online powerhouse Amazon, Pratt embraces the challenge. Recognizing that one of the main advantages of such competitors is price, Best Buy has re-calibrated its "lowest price guarantee". Now it covers best price anywhere – i.e. online or in-stores.

For Best Buy, stretching its former pricing model is another example of how the company is taking the data it has heard and acting on it in a way that matters to customers. Such pricing is possible because of Best Buy's volume buying power, which ties in well with customers' desire for choice. That means Best Buy is constantly adding product categories to its website every month, providing an expanded assortment of non-traditional items.

Share the Listening…down the Supply Chain

While the company doesn't manufacture its own products, it does contribute to the innovations of its suppliers by sharing (and facilitating) customer feedback with its own suppliers. They gather feedback from employees and customers on what is resonating in terms of product features and deliver that data to suppliers regularly.

"We're a nimble organization" says Pratt. Ultimately, that's because Best Buy has made listening intently a fundamental part of the company's strategy.

BUSINESS TRUTHS ABOUT IMPLEMENTING A LISTENING STRATEGY

- Define a set of business goals that will be aided by building a listening strategy.

- Define the audiences, communities or groups that you need to better undestand.

- Establish an "active listening policy" that outlines appropriate behaviours, e.g. those behaviours that respect the privacy concerns of the audiences you will be tapping into.

- Build in opportunities for conversation between two or more people/groups.

- Model a listening strategy across the company with involvement from the company's leader(s).

- Anticipate, and plan for, feedback that initially makes you/your company feel uncomfortable or angry.

Original BusinessCast Episode: http://bit.ly/BCBestBuy
13.52 minutes

CHAPTER 2

CHALLENGING THE NORM TO GAIN MARKET SHARE

Featuring Peter Aceto, President and CEO, ING Direct Canada

Peter Aceto is keenly aware that ING Direct Canada jumped into the business fray as the underdog. After all, it was competing with the business establishment: banks that had been building relationships and brand recognition throughout Canada for 150 years.

"As a challenger," he says, "we have to be fast, we have to be customer focused and we have to be innovative in order to be successful."

Bringing a New Take to an Old Product

In 2011, ING Direct introduced a new product, Thrive Chequing, a unique offering that allowed banking customers to save money by writing cheques. There are no transaction fees and the customer receives interest on the balance. At the same time, ING Direct offered Canadians a debit card to make it easier to access the chequing account. This was instantly at odds with the chequing products that long-established banks had brought to market. Instantly, ING Direct garnered attention, changed customer expectations, and established itself as a challenger.

To some of those within the financial sector, this product may have appeared to have been ill conceived but it was based on a deep understanding of how customers access their money in a "do it yourself" society. As Peter Aceto says, people are more willing "to do things online themselves, such as opening their own bank accounts and managing them online". This approach, and the resulting innovations, enabled the bank to reduce operating costs so they could offer customers what they truly want and need.

Engaging Employees and Customers

While bringing in to a mature market a new chequing product appeared to the banking establishment as a risky move, it was an example of ING Direct's proven approach of engaging all the relevant stakeholders in product development. Indeed, early in the process, ING Direct asked their own employees to build a product they would want themselves – a product that addressed those things they didn't like about conventional accounts. Then the product was made available to more employees and eventually to customers, who "field tested it" and provided their feedback. Aceto makes it clear that they didn't just decide to create a chequing account. Rather they asked the question: "What was the next thing Canadians needed that ING Direct could help them with?"

This process let all stakeholders take ownership in the product and become its enthusiastic ambassadors. Furthermore, by using this methodology, ING Direct can launch products when they are 90% finished and gather feedback before finalizing an offering.

Committing to Important Values

Making inroads to a mature market requires a commitment to understanding and connecting with market values. For example, according to Aceto, people understand that companies need to make money so they can succeed and grow – and this requires a commitment to openness and doing good things for the community. As he says, "The world is becoming more transparent. Employees and customers alike are expecting more from the companies they do business with and the companies they work for."

Keeping an Eye to the Future

Staying competitive in a mature market also means constantly having your antennae tuned to upcoming trends. According to Aceto, there are two key trends that need to be understood and monitored: the pace at which technology is shaping people's everyday lives and the evolving role that corporations play in society.

As ING Direct continues to penetrate mature markets, Aceto maintains a positive outlook, "We are living in an amazing time of change."

BUSINESS TRUTHS ABOUT GAINING MARKET SHARE IN A MATURE MARKET

- Conduct research to identify how your competitors and their products are perceived and valued by the market.

- Identify the fundamental values that your market wants you to "live and breathe" then develop products that embody those values.

- Use innovation methodologies that allow you to repeatedly validate your products.

- Monitor the industry's top trends — even those that may be disruptive to your own business and ways of thinking and operating.

Original BusinessCast Episode: http://bit.ly/BCINGDirect
14.21 minutes

CHAPTER 3

TAPPING INTO COMMUNITIES FOR AWARENESS AND SALES

Featuring Julie Cole, Co-founder and Vice-President, Mabel's Labels

It's easy to think of Julie Cole as a busy mom running a small business. But the reality is she is an astute businesswoman who has achieved a work-life balance that many would envy. Witness the success of Mabel's Labels, which was established in 2002 and continues to grow.

Mabel's Labels is a partnership of four women who fit the demographic of young working mothers of young children. Those young children shared a problem common to children everywhere – they were always losing things. Agreeing that the existing ways of labeling their children's belongings such as masking tape or permanent markers needed to improve, the four friends identified a gap in the market and the result was Mabel's Labels.

Word of Mouth Marketing

To bring a new product to market successfully means educating potential customers. Cole and her partners didn't have a big budget so they turned to "feet on the street" marketing, attending baby shows and spreading the word in their own communities. Young mothers only needed to see these labels to know they wanted them.

This was reinforced when the product was mentioned in Canadian Living magazine. The higher profile brought a spike in sales. More importantly, the company received a second increase in sales a few weeks later when word-of-mouth referrals created a new group of customers. Cole considers this groundswell of sales-generating referrals resulted from "Word of Mom" marketing.

Building Product Integrity

Although it's a simple concept, the product does what it says it will do – it labels items. The labels are dishwasher and microwave safe, so they can go on baby bottles, lunch boxes and snack containers. When kids go off to camp, the labels go on flashlights, clothes and sleeping bags.

The core benefit of the products is summarized in Cole's observation that, "Everything that goes out, returns." She asserts, "Children's "stuff" is expensive and the modest $20 cost to personalize and label items properly makes sure that items aren't lost."

Building a Product-Loyal Community

Cole and her partners have gone to great lengths to build and sustain a community around Mabel's Labels. She explains, "We know that moms don't want to buy from nameless, faceless strangers. They want to feel connected to, and trust, the brand." Part of the focus in building the community was to let customers know that the women behind the company are mothers like themselves who encounter the same daily challenges.

This easily relatable image and "personal" connection is reinforced through the company's ongoing social media activities. For instance,

Cole is active on Twitter and she writes a blog. She also contributes to blogs written by opinion leaders in the field of parenting. Cole was particularly pleased with the results of one blogger outreach initiative that targeted such "mom influencers". When a blogger talked about a child starting school, for example, Mabel's Labels would send her personalized labels and invite the blogger to do a giveaway contest on her blog. This led to thousands of readers learning about the product from trusted influencers.

Cole stresses that she's not always talking about the company or its products on social media. In fact, 80% of her social media commenting is about general issues of interest to parents. Efforts have paid off. Mabel's Labels' Facebook page has a community of over 60,000 people who actively talk about the company and its products, as well as share common experiences.

Expanding the Product Line

Mabel's Labels continues to extend its successful product line. The sticky label that survived the wash cycle was the original product. From there, the company developed shoe labels, clothing labels and bag tags. This was followed by a series of safety products with allergy alert labels. When attached to snack containers, these labels alerted teachers and daycare workers of potential reactions to peanuts and other foods.

Another safety hazard, having a child wander off in crowded places, has also been addressed with a label – a wrist band showing a parent's cell phone number. One grateful customer wrote to tell of a visit to Disneyworld. She had lost sight of her child and within thirty seconds someone called her cell phone to tell her, "We've got your son here."

Building a Community for the Leaders

Building a business with several partners creates a unique set of challenges. But the Mabel's Labels partnership has worked largely because of clarity of roles, clarity of vision, and clarity of commitment to their own community. When considering the company's success at growing the business while growing stronger as managers, Cole suggests the following:

- Establish shareholder agreements early in the relationship to avoid future misunderstandings.

- Spend time identifying each partner's expectations – particularly around responsibilities, obligations, and skill levels.

BUSINESS TRUTHS ABOUT LEVERAGING COMMUNITY FOR SALES

- Devote time and resources to build trust within any online or offline community.

- Identify and engage the leaders and influencers in the communities you are targeting.

- Focus on identifying ways that you can bring true value to a community rather than focus on how to sell into it.

- Manage your reputation within any community in order to build and protect it.

- To maintain a successful community, be authentic at all times.

- Devote resources to monitoring communities because they are always evolving.

Original BusinessCast Episode: http://bit.ly/BCMabelsLabels
14.27 minutes

CHAPTER 4

USING CUSTOMER CONFERENCES: THE ULTIMATE FEEDBACK TOOL

Featuring Eran Farajun, VP Business Development, Asigra Inc.

All successful businesses carve out ways to establish and sustain important points of differentiation. How can you ensure that your business and products are meaningfully different from your competitors?

According to Eran Farajun, VP Business Development of Asigra Inc., the answer is rooted in a deep understanding of customers and Asigra has a unique vehicle for making sure it's always connected with its customers. It's their annual customer conference.

Based in Toronto and in business for almost thirty years, Asigra provides cloud-based software to help mid-market and enterprise companies recover lost data from any device. Because lost data has a serious impact on business operations, it's imperative that it is recovered quickly and that's where Asigra comes in.

Although Asigra is one of the top rated cloud backup services in the world, end-users may not even recognize its name because the company doesn't deal directly with them. Asigra's customers are service providers who use the software to deliver cloud backup service to their customers. In other words, Asigra's customers consist solely of channel partners.

The Great Gathering

Once a year, Asigra's channel partners from around the globe come together in a single location for an event at which they are the focus. These channel partner customers get the chance to talk to Asigra as well as with each other. This event allows Asigra to share with their channel partners what they've learned about the market, provide competitive intelligence and give a sneak peak at the new ideas and technology the company is developing.

The conference – the largest of its kind for cloud backup service providers – serves the complex and varied needs of its attendees through four themed tracks: technology, marketing, sales and executive sponsorship. Approximately 400 channel partner customers gather from six continents to connect and give feedback at the multi-day event.

Usually it's the technical professionals from a channel partner who initially attends, but when they see the amount of information available on sales, marketing and management, they invite their colleagues from those areas to attend in subsequent years. By the third year, often the executive sponsor attends the event.

How to Run an Effective Customer Conference

For business leaders who are considering running their own customer conferences, Eran Farajun has three pieces of advice:

First, keep the audience "top of mind" and remember it's all about them. While it is free for attendees, they are devoting time to be at the event. Focus on what they want to get out of the conference – how to help them make their businesses better – rather than on trying to sell them more products or services.

Second, provide exceptional content. Attendees come to learn, so show them examples of best practices and give them opportunities to learn from one another. In addition to presenting its own employees, Asigra brings in third party speakers such as the luminaries from customers' industries, speakers knowledgeable in various facets of business, and amazing people who have created an impact in the market, all of whom the audience wouldn't normally be able to hear.

Finally, give them a great overall experience. The conference is primarily about the content, but the venue, the food and other details are also important. Make sure your employees are primed and ready to engage with customers. This takes some planning and coaching in advance, but it is well worth the investment.

Feedback Enables Differentiation

While feedback on the conference is important, Asigra wants deeper information from its channel partners. They seek product-related insights and potential improvements that lead to real ROI.

One unique aspect of the conference that attendees love is the hands-on lab, where they can see technologies Asigra is working on. The company reviews with them the business case for the technology and its functionality and channel partner customers give feedback. "That process has really come out of the partner conference each year," says Farajun. "It allows us to make sure the software we release into the market reflects what our customers and end-users want."

Of course, sometimes the feedback gathered at the event is negative.

Farajun looks at this from a "glass half full" perspective. "They want us to know they're not happy so that we can do something about it," he says. "If they didn't care, they wouldn't give us any feedback."

BUSINESS TRUTHS ABOUT MANAGING EFFECTIVE CUSTOMER CONFERENCES

- Create venues for gathering feedback rather than waiting for it to trickle in via phone calls, web forms, social media, or ad hoc surveys. Establish new and exciting opportunities to engage your customers and channel partners.

- Manage customer expectations by sharing which of their issues you will be addressing along with the timetables and challenges you face in resolving them.

- Embrace customer feedback and integrate it into your product development process. This results in better products and demonstrates that you care about your customers' needs.

Original BusinessCast Episode: http://bit.ly/BCAsigra
12.48 minutes

CHAPTER 5

SUCCEEDING IN A CROWDED MARKET: BEING UNIQUE IN THOSE THINGS THAT MATTER

Featuring Aaron Serruya, CEO, Yogurty's, Yogen Fruz, Jamba Juice Canada

According to Aaron Serruya, CEO of Yogurty's, Yogen Fruz, and Jamba Juice Canada, the North American marketplace has seen a recent explosion in the frozen yogurt business. However, to carve out a position as a market leader, Yogurty's has had to stay ahead of the competitors by taking – and sustaining – a unique approach.

Unique Market Segment and Product Mix

While many new entrants to the frozen yogurt market target customers aged four to seven, Yogurty's aims at yogurt lovers aged 12 to 39 – and they do this by striving to deliver an exceptional product and a great experience. By focusing on this market segment, as well as those people wanting healthy, yet decadent, fast food treats, Yogurty's is positioned well to take advantage of a potential market sweet-spot.

In his role as company visionary, Serruya is also the master franchisor for the Canadian operations of Jamba Juice, offering healthy, all-natural fruit smoothies and healthy alternatives (e.g. steel cut oatmeal, wraps, and sandwiches) to traditional fast foods. To take advantage of the synergies between the Jamba Juice products and those at Yogurty's, several joint franchises are being rolled out across the country. According to Serruya, the products offered by the two brands result in traffic patterns that complement one another.

Specifically, health-minded consumers visit Jamba Juice for breakfast or lunch. Then, as the daily traffic at Jamba Juice slows down by mid-afternoon, the foot traffic at Yogurty's picks up. With the two brands placed side-by-side, customers see Yogurty's when they visit Jamba Juice regularly. That allows people to become familiar with the frozen yogurt products in a convenient setting. The result: they return in the evenings for the frozen treats.

Unique Approach to Costing/Pricing

In parts of the United States, the frozen yogurt industry has reached the saturation point with independents and smaller chains exiting the business and leaving the market to a few companies.

If the same pattern plays out in Canada, Yogurty's could be one of the stronger players. This is due in part to its "sister company" Yogen Fruz – which has been selling frozen treats in Canadian malls and theatres for 25 years – being the largest manufacturer of frozen yogurt in Canada. Buying product for Yogurty's under the same umbrella creates an economy of scale, allowing it to maintain a high quality product at a favourable price. Serruya sees this price advantage, combined with the customer experience, as key to the company's long-term success in Canada.

Unique Operations

Yogurty's has also shown that meaningful differentiation extends beyond its offering into its own operations. For example, when Yogurty's started franchising in 2012, its competitors were opening stores rapidly – one at a time. In contrast, Yogurty's opted for a more thoughtful approach – opening several stores at once. While this took longer to coordinate, it also allowed the company to realize cost savings and observe its competitors' strengths and weaknesses.

Unique Staff

Fast food companies usually hire teenagers with little experience. Recognizing those with great skills and potential takes time. At Yogurty's, staff undergo several weeks of intense in-store training to learn the business and how to provide exceptional customer service. This type of training is only possible because Yogurty's is committed to transforming talented young people into powerful brand ambassadors.

BUSINESS TRUTHS ABOUT SUCCEEDING IN A CROWDED MARKET BY BEING UNIQUE IN THOSE THINGS THAT MATTER

- Define your market segments precisely including their knowledge and expectations about products similar to yours, purchase patterns, and obstacles to loyalty.

- Identify those potential points of distinction that matter most to your customers.

- Regularly monitor your competitors' actions (e.g. product launches, hiring activities, partnerships, pricing, promotions).

- Identify those areas of your operations that can contribute to being meaningfully different from your competitors.

Original BusinessCast Episode: http://bit.ly/BCYogurtys
13.03 minutes

CHAPTER 6

CREATING INNOVATIVE PRODUCTS

Featuring Simon Brightman, Co-Founder, AcceleratorU, (Former, Director of Product Management, Points.com)

Simon Brightman has been bringing new and innovative products to market for over a decade. But his experience and reputation extends well beyond his years. He writes for the Financial Post on all aspects of product innovation and is recognized across several industries as a product visionary. Today, his energies are devoted to helping entrepreneurs around the world harness their ideas and cost-effectively develop products that are enthusiastically embraced by the market.

Defining a Good Product

According to Brightman, "A good product is one that connects with its users and helps them better their lives even in small, simple ways." This definition applies regardless of the market or industry.

He offers three examples of good products:

In the financial services sector, ING Direct entered the world of large banks but they wanted to serve customers differently. They recognized that their customers wanted to deal with their money effectively on a daily basis. So they created a new product – a chequing account – that allowed them to easily access and organize their money without charging them for it.

In the online social media industry, LinkedIn has built a product that has helped professionals around the world build stronger business relationships.

In the telecommunications industry, Brightman cites Blackberry, whose core vision was to connect people to their businesses. Their initial products empowered people to do this by making it easy to access, review, write and send email messages safely and securely.

The Product Innovation Process

Brightman has led hundreds of products through varying innovation processes. He has often used the five-stage process effective across many industries known as the Product Development Life Cycle (PDLC). The five stages of the process include:

1. Ideation, or taking in ideas from various sources
2. Assessment of those ideas
3. Prioritization against certain metrics and objectives
4. Development
5. Launch

Iterating and Validating for Product Innovation

However, because PDLC is a very structured approach, companies can become too focused on the process itself rather than on the needs of a product's end-users. As a result, Brightman observes, some of the world's most innovative companies are adopting an iterative "Agile" approach to product innovation. This approach is characterized by:

1. Involving end-users through prototypes and pilots
2. Validating value throughout the development of products
3. Integrating immediate end-user feedback
4. Rapidly adapting product configurations

This approach quickly identifies the successful and unsuccessful features of a product, as described by its real end-users. It also facilitates ongoing communication with those people who will actually be buying and using the product.

Product Innovation Based on Clarity

According to Simon Brightman, ultimately, a company's ability to bring truly innovative products to market begins with clarity of vision. Leaders must have a clear vision and a path towards it; they must live it on a daily basis and continually communicate it to all stakeholders.

BUSINESS TRUTHS ABOUT PRODUCT INNOVATION

- Have a clear vision of what you want your product to do and how it will help users improve their lives.

- Develop product prototypes to reduce uncertainty, use multiple prototypes, and test your prototypes in "real life" contexts.

- Pilot your product before rolling it out to a large market.

- Build innovation through product iteration by introducing a version to the market, taking early feedback, and constantly adapting.

- Use customer purchase data to identify your customers' product adoption cycles before investing in future product feature enhancements, or retiring a product.

Original BusinessCast Episode: http://bit.ly/BCProductInnovation
11.57 minutes

SECTION SUMMARY

BUSINESS TRUTHS TO BUILD LOYALTY

BUSINESS TRUTHS ABOUT IMPLEMENTING A LISTENING STRATEGY

- Define a set of business goals that will be aided by building a listening strategy.

- Define the audiences, communities or groups that you need to better understand.

- Establish an "active listening policy" that outlines appropriate behaviours, e.g. those behaviours that respect the privacy concerns of the audiences you will be tapping into.

- Build in opportunities for conversation between two or more people/groups.

- Model a listening strategy across the company with involvement from the company'sleader(s).

- Anticipate, and plan for, feedback that initially makes you/your company feel uncomfortable or angry.

BUSINESS TRUTHS ABOUT GAINING MARKET SHARE IN A MATURE MARKET

- Conduct research to identify how your competitors and their products are perceived and valued by the market.

- Identify the fundamental values that your market wants you to "live and breathe" then develop products that embody those values.

- Use innovation methodologies that allow you to repeatedly validate your products.

- Monitor the industry's top trends – even those that may be disruptive to your own business and ways of thinking and operating.

BUSINESS TRUTHS ABOUT LEVERAGING COMMUNITY FOR SALES

- Devote time and resources to build trust within any online or offline community.

- Identify and engage the leaders and influencers in the communities you are targeting.

- Focus on identifying ways that you can bring true value to a community rather than focus on how to sell into it.

- Manage your reputation within any community in order to build and protect it.

- To maintain a successful community, be authentic at all times.

- Devote resources to monitoring communities because they are always evolving.

BUSINESS TRUTHS ABOUT MANAGING EFFECTIVE CUSTOMER CONFERENCES

- Create venues for gathering feedback rather than waiting for it to trickle in via phone calls, web forms, social media, or ad hoc surveys. Establish new and exciting opportunities to engage your customers and channel partners.

- Manage customer expectations by sharing which of their issues you will be a dressing along with the timetables and challenges you face in resolving them.

- Embrace customer feedback and integrate it into your product development process. This results in better products and demonstrates that you care about your customers' needs.

BUSINESS TRUTHS ABOUT SUCCEEDING IN A CROWDED MARKET BY BEING UNIQUE IN THOSE THINGS THAT MATTER

- Define your market segments precisely including their knowledge and expectations about products similar to yours, purchase patterns, and obstacles to loyalty.

- Identify those potential points of distinction that matter most to your customers.

- Regularly monitor your competitors' actions (e.g. product launches, hiring activities, partnerships, pricing, promotions).

- Identify those areas of your operations that can contribute to being meaningfully different from your competitors.

BUSINESS TRUTHS ABOUT PRODUCT INNOVATION

- Have a clear vision of what you want your product to do and how it will help users improve their lives.

- Develop product prototypes to reduce uncertainty, use multiple prototypes, and test your prototypes in "real life" contexts.

- Pilot your product before rolling it out to a large market.

- Build innovation through product iteration by introducing a version to the market, taking early feedback, and constantly adapting.

- Use customer purchase data to identify your customers' product adoption cycles before investing in future product feature enhancements, or retiring a product.

PART II:

BUSINESS TRUTHS TO GROW PROFITS

CHAPTER 7

KEEPING IT REAL

Featuring Dani Reiss, President and CEO, Canada Goose

In a world that has grown used to seeing even expensive name-brand merchandise manufactured in Asia, Canada Goose is an anomaly. In the early 2000s, when the exodus of clothing manufacturing from North America was helping international brands dramatically lower costs and increase profitability, Canada Goose made a conscious decision to keep its manufacturing force in Canada.

A Commitment to Keeping it Real

While other manufacturers continue to believe that cost-sensitive customers really don't care where their goods are made, Canada Goose has taken what many would see as a radically different approach. According to Canada Goose President and CEO, Dani Reiss, "You can't make a real Swiss watch in China. So why would you expect that you can make a real Canada Goose jacket in China?" For Canada Goose, that fundamental commitment to authenticity has fueled their rapid rise to the top of the winter clothing industry.

In fact, authenticity and determination helped Canada Goose truly distinguish itself from the competitors. It decided that to be a market leader it needed to "change the game" on competitors rather than competing with them on their terms. That's what Canada Goose did when it decided to continue manufacturing in Canada. They knew that if they could hold this position, they would find themselves in an industry where the competitors had left, leaving them with a point of distinction that could be turned into a powerful competitive advantage. That's exactly what happened.

Hiring for Real

At Canada Goose, maintaining authenticity is how they live, but making an authentic product in Canada is just the beginning. The culture of authenticity is part of the company's DNA and it shows in the way it hires people and manages performance.

When Reiss meets with applicants for managerial positions, he shares with them exactly how it is, potentially scaring them off by telling them they won't do well at Canada Goose unless they are comfortable at managing chaos. That way, people understand what they are getting into. When they do join the company, they find that Reiss was telling the truth - it is a fun place to work, fast-paced, and performance driven. But it's also hectic.

Building Products for Real

Even though "fashionistas" around the world can now be seen showing off the latest Canada Goose products – on city streets, in fashion magazines, and on fashion runways – Canada Goose remains true to its core and sees itself as a maker of functional clothing designed to keep people warm in cold weather.

The company's product line expansion reflects this focus by building on its core expertise, which is the use of natural down as powerful insulation. In fact, recognizing that not everyone needs the extreme insulation Arctic adventurers require, Canada Goose has created its own proprietary "Thermal Experience Index", which allows wearers to choose the type of warmth they need, whether it's a lightweight jacket for active pursuits or a field-tested parka for the coldest places on earth.

Listening to Real People

Canada Goose sees its customers as real people – as everyday heroes who strive for excellence. They climb mountains, lead expeditions, race dogsleds, and otherwise live extreme lifestyles and they do it all wearing Canada Goose clothing. They know firsthand what is essential in the clothes they wear in extremely cold conditions, so the company seeks their feedback when testing new products.

Garments that are being tested as potential new entrants for the product line are sent out to these real "Goose People", as well as to employees and other Canada Goose fans who are designated gear testers. They are asked for feedback, which is then built into the product development process. This lets the company validate products before they go into full production. Some items never make it to market because the gear testers have shown that for one reason or another they don't work. In other words, they don't pass the test of meeting the real needs of real people.

Marketing Real

When Dani Reiss took over Canada Goose, he realized there were amazing stories of people who wore the company's gear: people who lived and worked in the coldest places on earth. So he began to tell these stories of real people.

He saw, for example, that film crews working in Antarctica often wore Canada Goose gear. He pointed out to these crews that people who live in Antarctica wear Canada Goose jackets too. So, he asked the filmmakers, "Why not have them in front of the camera as well as behind?"

As it turned out, this was a critical moment in Canada Goose history, leading to its sponsorship of major film festivals around the world, including the Toronto International Film Festival and the Sundance Film Festival. Telling Canada Goose stories through film in this way magnified them and put the company's brand of authenticity in front of more people around the world.

The Real Patriot

The "Made in Canada" label has served Canada Goose well as it has expanded in the world marketplace. Reiss sees that Canadians are well positioned to compete globally because growing up in a multicultural society means having a much-desired understanding and appreciation for cultural diversity that is unique in the world.

But even so, successful international growth takes time. According to Reiss, going into a new marketplace for a year isn't enough. You must plan to be there for at least three years before you decide it hasn't worked. He also advises potential global players to pay close attention to pricing. The myriad international tax issues and import duties can easily lead a company to overprice its products or have too wide a spread between its prices in different markets.

The Real Family Business

Canada Goose is successfully managed by the third generation of the Reiss family, a status that many family businesses would envy. Reiss credits much of this success to the attitude of his father, who had allowed his son to run the business in his own way.

In fact, nobody was more surprised than Dani when he not only stayed in the family business, but grew it into the international success story it is today. As he says, "I never thought I could become passionate about parkas." But he found more than passion for parkas. He found a passion for authenticity and for a way to build that into a thriving company in a highly competitive and international industry. His advice to new generations of family businesses is not to join the business because it's expected of you, but because you believe that it is really who you are and who you want to be.

BUSINESS TRUTHS ABOUT KEEPING IT REAL

- Build your vision on deeply held values. Hold firmly to these values as they help establish a strong foundation for profitability and guide you to make difficult decisions.

- Articulate your competency – one that allows you to make a profit. Build on this competency so you are not pulled away from those things that you do exceptionally well and that sustain your profitability.

- Find something that you are truly passionate about and build it into your day-to-day business operations. It will help to carry you through the tough times that you will face when growing a company.

Original BusinessCast Episode: http://bit.ly/BCCanadaGoose
13.41 minutes

CHAPTER 8

BOOTSTRAPPING TO SUCCESS

Featuring Alex Savva, Co-founder, PharmaFreak

The Gap in the Market

Supplements form an important part of bodybuilding regimes. But for PharmaFreak's Co-founders Alex Savva and Don Gauvreau, available supplements were over-hyped and under-performing. So Savva, an avid bodybuilder and fitness industry advocate, and Gauvreau set out to make the strongest possible supplements that delivered on the promise of increasing strength. What was their strategy to achieve this ambitious goal? Bootstrap to success.

Bootstrapping by Leveraging First-hand Product Knowledge

To create an effective line of supplements meant working for two years with experts in the pharmaceutical and supplement industries. Fortunately, Gauvreau is one of the top formulators in the supplements industry. He knew what the industry studies were showing, what the best ingredients were, and what the most effective dosages would be.

However, before taking the product to market, the co-founders took a bold, yet measured step: they tested the product on themselves. "We made Ripped Freak for ourselves," says Savva, "because we weren't satisfied with other fat burners on the market."

Bootstrapping by Tapping Into the Target Market

PharmaFreak had an additional powerful advantage beyond deep product knowledge. They had very close ties with the target market. So they offered their initial product to their own athlete friends who are vitally interested in supplements and serve as a ready-made focus group. Using this first-hand and immediate market feedback, the co-founders decided to package and promote the supplement.

Using this same approach to product development, PharmaFreak produced their second product, Test Freak, a natural testosterone booster. As Savva says, "When the first batch is ready, we are the ones that are waiting for it. And because we are the target market, we know that if we are excited about a product that's coming out, our customers will be too."

Bootstrapping the Financing and Promotion

According to Savva and Gauvreau, PharmaFreak was built on passion – the co-founders love fitness and bodybuilding. They began with no money except their own personal credit. Because they didn't have the big advertising budgets of their competitors, they took a grassroots approach. "We hit every bodybuilding and fitness event we could," says Savva. "We were physically there, meeting and greeting people, spreading the word about our brand, and why our products are different and better than everything else."

Bootstrapping the Global Marketplace

Contrary to conventional thinking, Savva and Gauvreau do not actively seek out international partners because it takes time, resources and energies away from current operations. Rather, their strategy is to produce the best supplements for the North American market and let international partners come to them. This approach for bootstrapping the global market place – by not focusing on it – has worked and PharmaFreak is now a true Canadian export success story.

The company currently has fifteen products in its line, which is sold in over forty countries. The company's top markets are North America, Australia, New Zealand, South Korea, Europe and Indonesia. With attention to each territory, distributor and retailer, PharmaFreak monitors the success of its products in various markets.

BUSINESS TRUTHS ABOUT BOOTSTRAPPING TO SUCCESS

- Choose an industry you know well because it gives you the perspectives, values, networks and jargon that are required to run a profitable business and which are unique to each industry.

- While you build your business around something you are passionate about, direct time and responsibilities over the profitability of your business to a colleague and/or a trusted business advisor.

- Focus on short-term profitable successes in addition to long-term grand goals.

Original BusinessCast Episode: http://bit.ly/BCPharmaFreak
11.55 minutes

CHAPTER 9

STARTING LEAN, GATHERING MOMENTUM — THEN ITERATING

Featuring Derek Szeto, Co-founder, Dossiya

The Quick Inside Scoop

The core purpose of Dossiya, the brainchild of Derek Szeto, founder of Red Flag Deals, is to help busy professionals be more successful by providing required information about individuals and companies. But unlike the pervasive business social network LinkedIn, which requires energies and time to mine, Dossiya provides the inside scoop in a quick and relevant summary by spanning all online social media channels.

It includes, for example, Facebook photos, what their cover photos say about them, and information you have in common with another person that could be used as a conversation starter at an initial meeting. And because Dossiya is presented using a clean and simple design, it is accessible on a range of devices – essential for busy professionals and entrepreneurs who are often far away from their desks when they need the inside scoop on people and their companies.

The Dossiya software automatically assembles the basic information a sales person or executive needs but does so faster and more easily. It is designed to be consumed in less than three minutes. Adding to its power, the information gathered by Dossiya can separate business information and personal information.

Build Through Word-of-Mouth

Rather than establishing elaborate marketing processes, Szeto keeps his team lean. He understands word-of-mouth marketing from his previous entrepreneurial endeavours, such as Red Flag Deals, a couponing site he built and sold to the Yellow Pages Group. He believes Dossiya will grow in a similar, organic way, stating, "The tool is so useful that people will tell their colleagues and friends about it. This will establish it within particular groups. And like a snowball gathering momentum as it rolls down a hill, Dossiya will gradually build the critical mass that will lead to larger and faster promotion and growth."

In time, the business will operate on the "freemium" model that has been successful for many online offerings. In Dossiya's case, customers will be able to choose the service with little or no advertising for a nominally higher price than those who are content to receive advertising.

Adapt and Iterate

Szeto describes Dossiya as a "lean" startup which to him means "staying close to the customer". So rather than building a product and then using many marketing avenues to sell it, he starts by talking to customers about a particular concept he is exploring. Based on the feedback he gathers, Dossiya develops an initial solution and makes further changes or iterations based on hard data and soft data.

Since the company's growth momentum depends on gathering, analyzing and acting on hard data, his team is constantly monitoring new and recurring revenues, average value of its typical customers, and the number of reports requested or generated daily.

"The faster you iterate, the faster you are going to win your particular market," says Szeto. In essence, staying close to the customer allows you to deliver what the customer wants instead of maintaining a static vision of an ideal solution.

Szeto draws on one final piece of the puzzle to help him iterate quickly: an advisory board that consists of people with a diverse background who have real world industry expertise and insights. For Szeto, this board, which he draws upon for strategic rather than operational considerations, is his "ace in the hole".

BUSINESS TRUTHS ABOUT STARTING LEAN AND ITERATING FAST

- Build processes and technologies that allow you to gain real insights into what customers and would-be customers really want and need.

- Regularly re-examine preconceived notions of products, offerings and pricing/discounts — particularly if customers show no real interest in them.

- Constantly validate your financial and market assumptions with your management team, customers and advisory board.

Original BusinessCast Episode: http://bit.ly/BCDossiya
16.43 minutes

CHAPTER 10

CREATING A GREAT CULTURE, GREAT TEAMS AND GREAT PRODUCTS

Featuring Albert Lai, Co-founder and CEO, Big Viking Games

Albert Lai is the definitive serial entrepreneur. The Co-founder and CEO of Big Viking Games has started seven companies in the technology field and when asked what's common to them all, he responds enthusiastically, "They're all different!"

Like many other entrepreneurs before him, Albert Lai started each business because he wanted to solve a problem. Albert is a seasoned technology business leader and his companies focus on finding solutions to those problems through the innovative application of leading-edge and bleeding-edge technologies.

The New Canadian Technology Environment

Lai admits that just five years ago he took a lot of criticism for his publicly stated view that Canada was not the place to start a company, mainly because of the difficulty in raising capital.

Having been an active leader in the entrepreneur community, he is convinced that things have recently turned around for Canadian entrepreneurs. Now there are more Canadian early-stage investors, more institutional investors and more funds available for investment in all sorts of early-stage companies.

According to Lai, the greatest opportunities for technology-oriented entrepreneurs reside squarely in innovations that focus on leveraging mobile platforms. He observes, "The mobile platform is the source, and focus of, the biggest innovation revolution." Lai further focuses the direction of that growth in mobile innovation in one particular area: mobile games.

The good news is that Canada is positioned to capture a leadership position in this fast-growing technology niche. First, Canada has unprecedented amounts of government support. The only other country that comes close to Canadian levels of government support is Singapore, but it lacks the other component that makes Canada Lai's first choice: technical talent. Canada is among the three largest game development hubs in the world, five times the size of the U.S. industry on a per capita basis.

For these reasons, as well as its high standard of living, Lai maintains that Canada will be the home of the next billion dollar game company. "That's why I'm so excited about building a mobile game company right here in Canada," he says. "And for the first time, I would actually choose to start a company in Toronto as opposed to San Francisco."

Three Essential Qualities for Entrepreneurial Success

At the top of Lai's list of essential qualities for entrepreneurs to successfully tap into today's favourable business conditions is the ability to persist in the face of failure. "The ability to deal with failure and reflect on it honestly, to learn from it and bounce back from failure is a necessary ingredient to success," he says. As he points out, only the success stories become known and the failures don't get the attention they deserve.

His second required quality is the ability to identify and attract talent. He points out that while there is an abundance of opportunity in the technology field, there is a scarcity of truly talented technical people. As a result, it's critical that entrepreneurs can attract and keep the best people despite the high competition for talent. Because of that, Lai begins every new venture by focusing on creating a positive and innovative culture. He says, "A great culture means you will attract and retain great people and great teams. And these great teams will spawn great products."

The Big Misconception

Lai's third essential quality for entrepreneurs is the ability to operate in an uncertain environment. According to Lai, "You must be able to take risks, have faith in your vision and follow opportunities regardless of what others think." However, this quality has another side that can lead entrepreneurs down the wrong path, where all dissenting opinions, beliefs and data are ignored to the detriment of the idea or company.

In reality, it is difficult for entrepreneurs to realize and admit when they are going in the wrong direction and need to implement a "course correction". But success demands a fine balance between being bold, having faith in the vision, and taking advantage of the wealth of data and feedback that help to steer the right course for the business.

Lai has learned to dramatically reduce the risk of overlooking or under utilizing opposing, but valuable, viewpoints by conducting thorough research. He speaks to industry leaders as well as to potential customers, which enables him to rapidly test and validate ideas.

Use Technology for Research

So where does he do his research? He begins with the popular online investment community, Angel List, where anyone can access a network of companies and investors that might be interested in new ideas. He describes Angel List as "a LinkedIn or Facebook for angel investment" and recommends it as an efficient way of connecting companies to seed capital.

While keen on developing businesses in Canada, Lai also looks abroad for capital. He suggests some of the best places to look for those interested in funding specific segments: for software technology, San Francisco; for media technology, New York; for hardware technology, Boston.

BUSINESS TRUTHS ABOUT CREATING A GREAT CULTURE, GREAT TEAMS AND GREAT PRODUCTS

- Constantly challenge yourself about whether you are innovating to create something new or to address a real-world problem that people, businesses and communities will pay to solve.

- Devote time to recognizing, building, and re-configuring a corporate culture that will attract and retain the kind of people you need to generate industry-leading products/services.

- Expect, plan, budget, and structure for multiple "course corrections".

- Have faith in your vision while soliciting insights from trusted business advisers who will challenge you about the financial health and cultural cohesiveness of your business operations.

- Regularly review the traditional business success metrics as well as indicators that reveal whether your culture is enabling and inspiring the innovation needed for your business to be successful.

Original BusinessCast Episode: http://bit.ly/BCBigViking
13.24 minutes

SECTION SUMMARY

BUSINESS TRUTHS TO GROW PROFITS

BUSINESS TRUTHS ABOUT KEEPING IT REAL

- Build your vision on deeply held values. Hold firmly to these values as they help establish a strong foundation for profitability and guide you to make difficult decisions.

- Articulate your competency – one that allows you to make a profit. Build on this competency so you are not pulled away from those things that you do exceptionally well and that sustain your profitability.

- Find something that you are truly passionate about and build it into your day-to-day business operations. It will help to carry you through the tough times that you will face when growing a company.

BUSINESS TRUTHS ABOUT BOOTSTRAPPING TO SUCCESS

- Choose an industry you know well because it gives you the perspectives, values, networks and jargon that are required to run a profitable business and which are unique to each industry.

- While you build your business around something you are passionate about, direct time and responsibilities over the profitability of your business to a colleague and/or a trusted business advisor.

- Focus on short-term profitable successes in addition to long-term grand goals.

BUSINESS TRUTHS ABOUT STARTING LEAN AND ITERATING FAST

- Build processes and technologies that allow you to gain real insights into what customers and would-be customers really want and need.

- Regularly re-examine preconceived notions of products, offerings and pricing/discounts — particularly if customers show no real interest in them.

- Constantly validate your financial and market assumptions with your managment team, customers and advisory board.

BUSINESS TRUTHS ABOUT CREATING A GREAT CULTURE, GREAT TEAMS AND GREAT PRODUCTS

- Constantly challenge yourself about whether you are innovating to create something new or to address a real-world problem that people, businesses and communities will pay to solve.

- Devote time to recognizing, building, and re-configuring a corporate culture that will attract and retain the kind of people you need to generate industry-leading products/services.

- Expect, plan, budget, and structure for multiple "course corrections".

- Have faith in your vision while soliciting insights from trusted business advisers who will challenge you about the financial health and cultural cohesiveness of your business operations.

- Regularly review the traditional business success metrics as well as indicators that reveal whether your culture is enabling and inspiring the innovation needed for your business to be successful.

PART III:

BUSINESS TRUTHS TO SUCCEED AT EVERYTHING IN BETWEEN

CHAPTER 11

TRANSFORMING AN INDUSTRY

Featuring Julia Hartz, Co-Founder, Eventbrite

In 2006, the ticketing industry was the domain of one large agency that focused on selling tickets to large public events. At that time, Julia Hartz, Kevin Hartz and Renaud Visage, co-founders of Eventbrite, recognized an underserved market –small and medium sized events' organizers who had no cost-effective solution for organizing events and selling tickets.

Now, Eventbrite employs over 200 full-time staff and has expanded its San Francisco-based operations to include an office in London, England.

Establishing a Strong Foundation Before Seeking Capital

Eventbrite is the poster child for bootstrapping a business. For the first two years, they focused on their product and their customers by doing all the work themselves. This helped them stay financially viable and let the team learn the nuts and bolts of their business and the industry they were about to transform.

Then in 2009, when the company was breaking even, Eventbrite began courting potential investors. However, their pursuit for cash was not their primary reason for seeking outside capital. Rather, they made this strategic decision because they had developed a clear vision of where they wanted to take the business and what they needed in order to get there.

But, to establish a favourable venture capital investment deal in just 14 days with world-renowned Sequoia – who would believe that was possible for a relatively new business? To successfully achieve this goal, Eventbrite had by this time developed a track record of tangible results (i.e. measurable growth, stable operations, realistic projections and a validated value) that gave it the leverage to find the right partner rather than take the first deal offered to them. At the same time, co-founder Kevin Hartz had built credibility and strong relationships with potential investors.

Maintaining a Long-Term Vision

When entrepreneurs bring in outside capital, often it's with a view to eventually selling their shares for a profit and stepping away. That was never Eventbrite's intention. In the minds of the co-founders, selling would have been a failure. Says Julia Hartz, "We don't want to start a new company. We're focused on making Eventbrite a long-term success and being with the company until they (Sequoia) show us the door." Fortunately for Eventbrite's growing and loyal customer base, Sequoia also shares this long-term view.

Focusing on One Key Product

Eventbrite has taken an unusual route to success in that it hasn't sought multiple streams of revenue. As Ms. Hartz enthusiastically states, "For better or for worse, we focus on optimizing just one revenue stream. We charge a per-ticket fee." That fee is 2.5% of the transaction price plus 99 cents. Sometimes the event organizer pays the additional fee, sometimes the attendee – but never both.

Adopting a "one revenue stream" approach is contrary to the vast majority of software-as-a-service companies that look for several different sources of recurring revenue. That's because the founders don't aspire to be a traditional software-as-a-service provider. They aspire to create a marketplace that transforms how people organize events and think of the ticketing transaction. This vision allows them to concentrate on removing any friction from the transaction. The result: customer on-boarding is faster along with an enviable inventory of events on their site. This in turn provides a clear value proposition to customers.

While Eventbrite's database includes an array of user and behavioural information that could bring other streams of income through data mining, Ms. Hartz is more intrigued by its possibilities as a source for enhancing the core product offering. For example, the company's data team is focused on ways that the data can recommend events and make the discovery of other events a better experience for customers.

Eventbrite's one product approach has been embraced. Its customers are rewarding the transformative industry pioneer with their ongoing business. Specifically, Eventbrite facilitated over $300 million (US) in ticket sales in 2011 and doubled that in 2012. With Eventbrite's help, its event-organizing customers managed half-a-million events worldwide in 2011 alone, and sold over 20 million tickets to those events. Those numbers are expected to increase exponentially.

Staying Ahead of the Competition

With the growing acceptance of online transactions, the industry has been transformed and potential competitors are nipping at Eventbrite's heels. But the company is ready for them.

Case in point: While it may be easy to create an online transaction model, especially by leveraging an array of available payment processors, it takes a sophisticated infrastructure to stay ahead of make-or-break challenges. This includes ensuring protection for all parties in a transaction from being victims of fraud. Eventbrite is far ahead of the competition in this area because of the work it has done over the years to guard its operations and customer data.

Taking the Company Global

Customer behavioural data revealed that 20% of Eventbrite's ticket sales came from outside the U.S., and much of that activity was in London. Therefore, London became the base from which to tackle the European market.

Of course, Europe is not a single market, but many different countries, each with its own focus and ways of doing business. While London is not the cheapest city in Europe, nor does it have the greatest tax incentives, it has other advantages. According to Ms. Hartz, "It's a hotbed of culture and event activity. That helps us to understand what kind of leverage we can use in Europe and how we can grow our brand."

With its industry leadership position and new presence in Europe, Eventbrite is poised for growth. And according to Ms. Hartz, to do that effectively, they must remain "acutely observational" in order to be ready for, and face head-on, any challenges the technology or the competition brings.

BUSINESS TRUTHS ABOUT TRANSFORMING AN INDUSTRY

- Focus on establishing strong business operations while learning the industry's current rules and inherent dysfunctions.

- Secure injections of capital only when you have a strong transformational vision and strategy.

- Use your customers, analysts, and media insiders to help you identify a unique value proposition that will keep you ahead of traditional competitors.

- Focus on building your company with people who are only satisfied with making transformative change.

- Implement processes that allow you to monitor and assess business risks because introducing real transformation to an industry is accompanied by great potential as well as great risks.

Original BusinessCast Episode: http://bit.ly/BCEventbrite
15.32 minutes

CHAPTER 12

FINDING AND KEEPING THE RIGHT EMPLOYEES

Featuring Dave MacDonald, CEO and President, Softchoice

For seven years in a row, the Great Places to Work Institute has named Softchoice, a leading North American provider of technology solutions and services, as the Best Workplace in Canada. According to Dave MacDonald, CEO and President of Softchoice, that was never the goal. Rather, winning the award "is an outcome of a culture that says that people are your most important resource and lives it."

Finding and Keeping the "Right" Employees

Creating and sustaining a corporate culture that truly emphasizes people starts with hiring a certain kind of person. MacDonald has observed that finding and hiring people that will truly thrive in the Softchoice culture is always a challenge – regardless of the state of the Canadian economy. However, when your company is recognized as a great place to work, your employee acquisition costs decrease. Of course, when the economy heats up, the focus shifts to keeping great people because the presence of more available opportunities naturally increases employee turnover.

Softchoice is actively using Facebook, LinkedIn and Twitter to recruit employees, given the age and technology-savvy demographic they are targeting. They also maintain a Corporate Social Responsibility blog (http://blogs.softchoice.com/csr/) which demonstrates the company's values and its philanthropic activities. MacDonald says, "This is fundamental to what young people are looking for today, so it's front and centre to who we are. That makes us a more attractive place to come to work."

A Culture That Considers the Whole Person

Softchoice looks for people who are excited about working in technology, so for the most part that means they are younger, innovation-focused and open to learning. Softchoice helps such employees grow into the business, providing them with the skills, opportunities and processes to become exceptional professionals. At the same time, the corporate culture encourages everybody to bring their whole self to work. In fact, Softchoice recognizes that people have a life that is outside of work and that the division between work and non-work isn't always in the best interest of employees or the company. MacDonald states, "When people come through the door to the office, the last thing we want them to do is feel they have to shut off their personal lives."

To further engage its employees, Softchoice goes to great lengths to make sure they understand the business. To that end, Softchoice holds a monthly call for all employees where they are given an update on what is going on with the business and the industry, and what needs to be accomplished during the next thirty days.

Unlike many other employers, Softchoice encourages employees to check their Facebook and other social media at work. Of course, they have a well-developed social media policy in place to help employees do this responsibly.

While Softchoice, as an organization, is more youthful than many companies, it also has senior talent with the experience to optimize the business. Special effort is made to ensure the generations are well integrated and work together. At the end of the day, whether it is age, race, religion or gender, diversity is valued at Softchoice. "Diversity of thought is really an important element of where we are going as an organization and it helps us to make better decisions," says MacDonald.

Focusing on Business-Related Human Resources Metrics

Softchoice is always tracking and managing business-related Human Resources metrics. For instance, they benchmark against themselves while tracking employee tenure and attrition. They also measure themselves against competitors on dimensions of employee churn and productivity.

At the same time, Softchoice recognizes career advancement as an important tool for individual and company growth. As such, they define career paths carefully and provide structured performance feedback to all employees throughout the year.

At the end of the day, says MacDonald, "We help people feel they are progressing which is the number one determinant of retention". Because it lives this commitment every day, Softchoice has hit upon a winning formula for retaining the right people.

BUSINESS TRUTHS ABOUT FINDING AND KEEPING THE RIGHT EMPLOYEES

- Build employee loyalty by including everyone in key organizational developments and announcements.

- Unleash the potential of people by first taking the time and effort to understand the value they can bring to the company.

- Regularly monitor Human Resources metrics that have an impact on business.

- Develop policies and processes so that people can harness social media for the satisfaction of employees and the good of the company.

- Implement an internal communications plan including tools and processes that encourage employees to feel part of a company-wide community.

- Implement a performance management program that involves everyone.

- Share with employees stories of success that strengthen the corporate culture.

Original BusinessCast Episode: http://bit.ly/BCSoftchoice
12.44 minutes

CHAPTER 13

MANUFACTURING SUCCESS: IT'S ALL ABOUT CONTROL

Featuring Claudia Harvey and Wendy Johansson, Co-founders, Dig It Handwear

Dig It Handwear is a business success story that was born out of a gap in the market that nobody else recognized. In 2007, Claudia Harvey and Wendy Johansson developed a revolutionary protective gardening glove. The Dig It Handwear product has a reinforced pillow-top protector inside the glove which prevents nails from pressing up against the glove. No friction means safe, manicured nails. Despite its novelty and practicality, Dig It Handwear could have remained a small local business, but the co-founders knew they had created a new product category that could capture the imagination of a wide market.

Manufacturing

With initial low sales volumes of their handwear, Harvey and Johansson used the services of a third-party manufacturer which outsourced the work to partners overseas. They chose a manufacturing partner that had been in business for 70 years and knew the glove and safety industry well. This was key to the company's initial success.

In fact, Harvey advises businesses only consider manufacturing partners with relevant industry experience. "Make sure your manufacturer knows your market particularly when launching your initial product," she says. Harvey also emphasizes the importance of communicating strongly, consistently and clearly with your outsourcers to make sure they create what you want.

After a year of operations, the co-founders realized they did indeed have a viable business and they wanted to have complete control over it. However, by using an outsourcer, they didn't have the control over the quality and turnaround times that were required by customers and other key stakeholders.

The co-founders decided it was time to build their own manufacturing team and tap into a different network of factories, so they established relationships with overseas manufacturers themselves. While initially taxing, this saved them time and energy. Having lived through that experience, they have three pieces of advice for any entrepreneur who must rely heavily on manufacturing operations:

- Conduct thorough research about product pricing – i.e. what competitors are offering, how it will impact sales, and how your price will assist in fueling your ability to conduct further innovation.

- Get to know your manufacturer extremely well. Go to different factories before choosing a partner, because you have to have confidence that they can, and will, deliver.

- Keep your eyes open to the human rights standards you want associated with your brand. When you are on site at the manufacturing facilities, pay attention to how they treat their employees, which reveals their code of ethics.

Entering the Dragons' Den

In the beginning, Dig It had a single product so it was important to focus their energies. As a result, they worked directly with small retailers and promoted through industry trade shows. But like most intrepid entrepreneurs, the co-founders wanted more; they wanted to grow their brand.

Harvey and Johansson decided on the potentially risky strategy of taking their product on CBC's business pitch series, The Dragons' Den. They realized this could backfire if they didn't present their case well, but felt the brand exposure would be worth the risk.

For them it paid off; they secured a deal with investor Kevin O'Leary, which was a turning point for the business. The profile they garnered on the show resulted in new sales and by leveraging new investment capital and O'Leary's networks, they strengthened distribution throughout national hardware and gardening retailers.

The Big Box Strategy

At this point, the co-founders of Dig It knew they had to make the most of their increased success. They targeted the all mighty "big box" chain retailers by applying for the Innovation for Sustainability program – a partnership between the Ontario Government and Home Depot. The result: their product was tested in three stores.

Their subsequent success brought them a national program at Home Depot where they earned real estate on standalone displays rather than having to fight for shelf space with other gloves.

During this process, the co-founders learned that their product was not as "retail friendly" as it could have been because the product's packaging prevented would-be customers from trying on the gloves. So once again, the partners took control. They went back to their manufacturer to create new packaging that allowed the gloves to be displayed and tried on without wear-and-tear on the product or the display.

The conclusion: With manufacturing and distribution partners, get to know them well and make sure that they can be held accountable.

BUSINESS TRUTHS ABOUT MANUFACTURING AND RETAIL DISTRIBUTION

- Manage the manufacturing and distribution of your products. If you don't have the required skills to do so, hire someone who does.

- Because protecting your brand is your responsibility, stay aware of the processes involved in manufacturing, distributing and selling your products.

- Get your products into a store where you can test its performance over time.

- Refine the packaging, the message, and the product itself until it performs well.

- Ensure your distribution partners know how and when to present your product in their promotional materials.

- Set specific goals for evaluating the effectiveness of your manufacturing, distribution and promotional partners.

Original BusinessCast Episode: http://bit.ly/BCDigIt
16.43 minutes

CHAPTER 14

RENTING OR BUYING YOUR BUSINESS PREMISES: MAKING THE RIGHT DECISION

Featuring Dianne Usher, President, Toronto Real Estate Board Vice-President and Division Manager, Royal LePage Real Estate Services Ltd., Johnston & Daniel Division

Grappling with the Common Scenarios

When it comes to investing in a physical premises for conducting day-to-day business operations, all business owners need to keep their options open.

For example, if your business isn't growing at the forecasted speed, you need to explore ways of cost-effectively reducing your office space size or shifting its location. On the other hand, rapid growth translates into the need for more space, potentially with short notice.

These very common and opposing scenarios point to the benefits of renting. As a renter of your business premises, it is easier to expand your space, contract it or move out. However, renting also has its disadvantages. For example, the inclusion of a put-back or destruction clause in a commercial lease means that upon leaving the space you must return it to the same state as when you took possession, regardless of the costs involved.

The growing availability of commercial condos, duplexes and small office spaces is causing business owners to consider the value of ownership. Dianne Usher, President of the Toronto Real Estate Board and Vice-President and Division Manager, Royal LePage Real Estate Services Ltd, Johnston & Daniel Division, agrees that this a legitimate option. Whether the premises are condo or freehold, and regardless of the nature of the business, if a business experiences a cash shortage, owners can leverage the equity they have in the physical premises to help finance the business. As Usher suggests, regardless of your business' success, you do indeed have value in real estate equity.

Recognizing Geographic Differences

In a country the size of Canada, there are wide variations in the local business, social and real estate demographics. To ensure that owners make the right buy/rent decision, Usher strongly recommends conducting research to make sure that local social and economic growth translates into real opportunities for your business and the value of its real estate. Specifically, determine if the regional market is built on a diverse set of industries and a growing infrastructure. When that it is the case, purchase investments are wiser. In contrast, if a market relies solely on one industry or one large employer, renting space is more prudent.

Using the Right Advisors

Usher further recommends that business owners draw upon their business plans, developed with the assistance of financial advisors who can analyze the market conditions. Given the complexity – and potential risk – of making the correct rent/buy decision, she underlines the importance of using professional advisors, including: lawyers with expertise in real estate laws, real estate tax, and business; CPAs - chartered professional accountants, who are familiar with rental and purchase transactions; mortgage brokers who have a wide network of lenders; and commercial/industrial real estate agents, who are familiar with the geographic areas you are considering and the nature of your business.

Another factor that's becoming more prevalent is the need for environmental assessments. Many types of land appear affordable, but the municipality or other levels of government may require remediation work to address environmentally sensitive issues. The land might be contaminated, for example, or it may be adjacent to waterways or hydro fields. These kinds of environmental aspects affect your bank's willingness to finance a mortgage.

BUSINESS TRUTHS ABOUT DECIDING TO RENT OR BUY YOUR BUSINESS PREMISES

- Use your business plan's projections for revenue, cash flow, human resources, client retention and I.T. to determine your needs for a business premises.

- Draw upon your team of accounting, legal, and real estate experts to develop a handful of risk/benefit scenarios for renting or purchasing a business premises.

- Reach out to the local Board of Trade or Business Association to get an overview of your community's growth.

Original BusinessCast Episode: http://bit.ly/BCRentOrBuySpace
12.45 minutes

CHAPTER 15

WORKING WITH A PR AGENCY TO TURN YOUR BRAND INTO NEWS

Featuring Alyssa Lioutas and Jennifer Love, Partners in Duet Public Relations

Choosing Your PR Firm

Your public relations firm can be a valuable asset and contribute significantly to your business' success so it is vital that you choose your firm carefully.

Your agency represents your brand, say Alyssa Lioutas and Jennifer Love, the founders and Partners of Toronto-based PR agency Duet. They provide some key considerations when choosing a PR agency:

- Clarify who at the agency you will be working with because it's often not the same person who sells you on the agency.
- Request case studies of the work the agency has done with businesses similar to yours.
- Spend enough time with them to get a sense of their competence and integrity.
- Speak to their clients and ask them to identify the measurable impact the agency has produced for them.

Managing Your Resources with Your Agency

While it can be worthwhile for companies to engage a PR agency, Liotas recommends to business leaders, "Make sure your capacity is in place to handle the potential upswing in media, customer, or investor interest that can accompany an effective media-building campaign. Otherwise, increased profile can have unwanted consequences."

Furthermore, Lioutas adds, "It takes commitment to work with a PR agency particularly since you will need to educate them about the uniqueness of your brand so that they can represent it well." Developing compelling stories that your PR professional can publicize takes time, yet it is absolutely essential to the success of any PR campaign.

In the interests of saving money, business owners and other leaders often try to do things themselves that are best left to professionals, including PR. The Duet partners claim, "Enthusiastic, savvy and well-intentioned entrepreneurs often think that because they are effective at running their business, they will be good at promoting it. Unfortunately, they haven't devoted the time to build media relationships and it is those relationships that really are at the core of successful campaigns."

Keep in mind that PR firms traditionally favour retainers. However, there are increasing pressures on agencies to accommodate other payment models such as project-based payment or results-based pricing. Choose a payment model that fits your familiarity with working with PR professionals. When you are confident that they have a track record of demonstrating relevant results and value, that's when it could make sense to consider the retainer model.

Evaluating Your PR Agency

Once you've chosen your PR agency, the Duet partners recommend that you monitor business results regularly, checking in at least quarterly. Your positive media exposure should grow along with those business metrics that you tie to increased media exposure.

If you are using a PR agency to build or strengthen your brand's reputation with a particular audience, you can measure success using a wide range of tools and techniques. Ask your agency to build in validating things like:

- The degree to which sample members of your target audience recognize your brand's name/products (i.e. unaided and assisted recall)

- The positive/negative associations members of your targeted audience have of your brand's name/products (i.e. sentiment)

Because of the ability to cost-effectively collect and measure this type of information, be very wary of PR agencies that fall back on the ill-defined goal of "getting your name out there".

BUSINESS TRUTHS ABOUT WORKING WITH A PR AGENCY TO TURN YOUR BRAND INTO NEWS

- When selecting a PR agency, you are largely purchasing their network of relationships with members of the media that speaks to your target audiences.

- Ask your potential PR agency to provide proof that they have indeed established relationships with members of the media that are relevant for you to leverage.

- Tie business metrics to your PR agency's activities so that you have meaningful ways for determining the value they provide.

- Allocate time to managing and monitoring your PR agency.

- To optimize your PR spend, explore those agencies that embrace package pricing or outcome pricing rather than hourly pricing.

- Research how the PR agency leverages media. The most competent agencies are adept at using today's technologies to build press for their clients.

- Enable your PR agency to be effective by providing them with newsworthy stories/content. In other words, effective PR is not about distributing marketing or sales messages through media channels.

Original BusinessCast Episode: http://bit.ly/BCDuet
15.42 minutes

CHAPTER 16

BUILDING STRATEGIC ALLIANCES THAT WORK

Featuring Phil Hogg, President, Association of Strategic Alliance Professionals Toronto

If you go to a Toronto Maple Leafs hockey game, you will notice an unusual phenomenon: competing telecommunication giants Rogers Communications and Bell Canada sharing the advertising and promotion space. That's because they formed a strategic alliance to purchase Maple Leaf Sports and Entertainment.

According to Phil Hogg, President of the Association of Strategic Alliance Professionals, Toronto Chapter, this is typical of the growing number of strategic alliances among companies that may have been, and continue to be, fierce competitors in their core businesses.

He cites a few other high profile alliances: IBM, Bell Canada and Cisco Systems worked on a joint technology project; the Royal Bank of Canada and the Bank of Montreal's joint venture, Moneris Solutions; and General Motors' partnership with the French automaker Peugeot to manufacture various components and modules.

Credit card giant Visa has formed a strategic alliance with Intel to develop e-commerce solutions for consumers in both developed and developing countries. In this case, Visa brings to the table its expertise in payment processing, account holder authentication and its global network, while Intel brings its expertise in chips and communications.

Such alliances are being announced every day. "It's not a question of whether one should establish a strategic alliance," says Phil Hogg, "but really when and with whom."

Effective Alliances Fill Needs for All Partners

Typically, strategic alliances allow individual partners to do things they could not do on their own. In the case of Bell Canada and Rogers, being in the telecommunications field and owners of media assets, both have an insatiable appetite for content. Neither one alone had the appetite to purchase Maple Leaf Sports and Entertainment, but by joining together they can take advantage of this rich source of media content.

If the content hadn't been secured by Bell and Rogers jointly, it's conceivable that Maple Leaf Sports could have established its own television network, which would have been a blow to both Bell and Rogers.

Why All These Strange Bedfellows?

According to Hogg, 40% of the revenue of Fortune 1000 corporations in the U.S. is generated by alliances. Twenty years ago, this figure was just 3 - 6%. This rapid and tremendous growth has been spurred by major changes in the commercial environment.

First, the movement towards a global marketplace creates a huge appetite for sales and distribution alliances in foreign markets. A Canadian company, for example, may want to sell its goods and services in Asia, or a U.S. company in South America. In either case, they will increase their success by pairing up with a local strategic partner.

Another factor is the dramatic growth of Internet-based communications that spurs consumer demand for sophisticated products. Considering the hardware and software often required to deliver these products, increasingly no single company is capable of developing, manufacturing, distributing and promoting the sought-for product. As a result, companies enter into strategic alliances to share resources, insights and data.

Sometimes It Ends in Divorce

According to Hogg, three elements make or break a strong alliance: strategic fit, operational fit and chemistry. However, sometimes alliances don't work out and that's okay. What may happen over time is that one of the three elements changes.

Seeking Out a Strategic Alliance Partner

Companies have only three ways to achieve growth: build, buy and ally. In other words, they can build by growing organically; they can enter into a merger or acquisition; or they can ally themselves with a strategic partner.

While all three strategies have their advantages, depending on the situation, Hogg points out that alliances allow quick entry into new markets and can reduce the associated risks. With a strategic alliance, you can borrow another company's assets, resources, capabilities, connections and knowledge. You can also learn from the other company's mistakes rather than making your own. Alliances can be profitably formed in marketing and sales, distribution, product development or research and development.

Hogg recommends any enterprise considering a strategic alliance should tap into alliance best practices for managing the alliance life cycle. Doing so can increase the short- and long-term success of a strategic alliance.

BUSINESS TRUTHS ABOUT ESTABLISHING AND SUSTAINING STRATEGIC ALLIANCES

- Before looking for a strategic alliance partner, make sure you can demonstrate that: (i) your financials are well documented; (ii) your profitability or revenue is trending upwards; (iii) your leadership team is committed to staying; (iv) you have invested in new products, new technologies or new markets; and (v) you have a clear sense of your company's core strengths and weaknesses.

- Make sure your potential alliance partner is a strategic fit, an operational fit and a cultural fit.

- "Test the waters" with a potential alliance partner. For example, conduct a time-limited and low-risk project where you can see how well you work together.

- Prior to entering any alliance, identify what success means. For example, success might be a specific number of introductions to new prospects, the amount of money saved on a joint initiative, or the total new revenues generated during a particular time period.

- Success will ultimately be defined by three goals – one that you set for your company, one your alliance partner sets for their company, and a jointly-defined goal that both of you will monitor.

- Regardless of the alliance's goal, make sure that you have the means to measure it.

Original BusinessCast Episode: http://bit.ly/BCStrategicAlliances
14.13 minutes

CHAPTER 17

PREPARING FOR EXPONENTIAL GROWTH

Featuring P. Bruce Hunter, CEO and President of Lighthouse 360

Entrepreneurs often launch a business with the goal of freeing themselves from the bureaucracies that are an unfortunate byproduct of big companies. However, when they are successful, business owners and leaders may find they are being slowed down and frustrated by the same kinds of bureaucratic processes and thinking they had sought to avoid.

That's what Bruce Hunter, CEO and President of Lighthouse 360, explores in his new book, The Success Cage: You've Built a Business That Owns You -- Now What?

Having worked with hundreds of business owners across North America, he has found an important pattern. The early years of a business are filled with the passion and the thrill of building something new. As time progresses, the business transforms itself into something more predictable. But according to Hunter, "Behind closed doors, entrepreneurs often confess that their business has grown in a different direction or at a pace much faster than had been expected. The outcome: they feel at a loss as to which way to turn."

The Entrepreneur's Dilemma

The fundamental problem, according to Hunter, is that the type of person who builds a company – along with the associated skills, goals, patience and mentality – is fundamentally different from those people who excel at managing a complex organization. They are builders and creators, with little time or patience for process. Yet as the business becomes more complex, it requires a new set of skills and infrastructure to continue to progress. As a result, there comes a time when even the most accomplished entrepreneur needs help in building the systems, processes, and human resources capable of evolving the business.

According to Hunter, there are three possible scenarios for businesses at this stage:

- The business may be re-sized, either by accident or by design, into something an owner can manage.

- The owner continues to try to manage the growth alone, usually resulting in stagnation, deterioration, collapse, or sale.

- The owner recognizes the situation and seeks outside help to chart a new path and infrastructure for the business; a structure which sees new leadership of the day-to-day operations of the business.

The Success Cage

In The Success Cage: You've Built a Business That Owns You -- Now What?, Hunter focuses in the first part of the book on typical organizational growth stages. While every business has a DNA that is unique, all proceed through five stages of growth, regardless of the industry or nature of business. Each stage has different characteristics, and organizational and leadership needs. Knowing where you are on this growth continuum is a critical step in understanding how to be successful in your current stage and what is needed at the next stage. Hunter provides a checklist to help business owners determine which stage they are in. This helps them make the right kind of plans and provides the leadership needed to evolve to the next growth stage.

Hunter also provides guidance on transforming the company from one that requires the owner's direct day-to-day management to one that can function more independently and predictably. This, according to Hunter, is the "hands-free" business where the owner is liberated from their "success cage" and is empowered to return to what they do best – building businesses.

The transformation starts with the owner taking a series of in-depth questionnaires to help pinpoint their personal and organizational preferences, behaviours, and dispositions. These are supplemented with a set of practical and market-tested tools.

Evolving from Entrepreneur to Executive

The skills and psychology of those who create and build new enterprises are very different from those who excel in managing much larger, complex organizations. Making the transition from one to another forms the biggest hurdle for businesses moving from adolescence to maturity.

To run a successful early-stage company, an owner needs to have the qualities and mindset of an entrepreneur. Hunter identifies the five essential entrepreneurial traits as being: persistence, extroversion, self-orientation, tolerance for risk, and open-mindedness or curiosity. Hunter observes that those traits actually work against the entrepreneur in transitioning to a larger, more sophisticated operation.

Executives have their own mindset. They need to be adept at transforming autocratic, closely-managed organizations into ones that are more broadly led. During the transformation, informal systems, management by intuition, and some resident personnel need to be replaced with fact-based data, disciplined processes, and different skills.

Planning and Delegating

A consistent challenge for a company transitioning from entrepreneur-led to executive-led is that the business owner, does not want, or know how, to delegate. To help them over this hurdle, Hunter provides a unique version of the one-page planning system.

Instead of including the company's vision, mission and values, Hunter's plan starts with a clear destination towards which the leader drives the company. The rest of the plan is devoted to identifying the critical projects, ownership, and timing that is needed to reach the destination.

To promote delegation, a key feature of this one-page business plan is that the owner must not appear to be in charge of any of the day-to-day activities. This compels the owner to delegate responsibilities – essential to building a self-sustaining organization. That means allowing people to perform and then holding them accountable for their performance.

BUSINESS TRUTHS ABOUT PREPARING FOR EXPONENTIAL GROWTH

- Determine whether you have the interest, skills, and mindset to lead a company that aspires to evolve beyond its current stage.

- Work with an outside consultant or Board of Advisors to help you identify the day-to-day "symptoms" of a business that is stuck in any one stage of growth.

- Work with an outside consultant or Board of Advisors to identify the skills and resources required to build systems and processes that enable the business to evolve from its current growth stage.

- Define short- and long-term goals for the company that can be tracked.

- Help people become successful by delegating responsibility and holding them accountable for their performance.

Original BusinessCast Episode: http://bit.ly/BCSuccessCage
12.37 minutes

CHAPTER 18

LEVERAGING THE POWER OF VIDEO

Featuring Mark Campbell, Account Director, VMG Cinematic

With the growing affordability and ease of online video-making, business owners are increasingly looking to produce and distribute product videos on sites such as YouTube, Vimeo and Viddler. While such efforts can be worthwhile, it's important to have realistic expectations about what these marketing tools can yield.

According to Mark Campbell at VMG Cinematic, business owners and leaders cannot maintain the former "build it and they will come" approach to online video.

Video Is Just Part of the Picture

According to Campbell, video production is considerably more effective when it's part of an aligned marketing plan. That means, before diving in, it's important to define specific objectives, budgets and measures of success.

For example, if your product is complex, videos that demonstrate its functionalities and features can make it easier to understand. Such videos can be used to market a product as well as to raise investment capital. Showing video demos online can also greatly reduce customer service expenses. For instance, instead of having your customers calling your 1-800 number, they can select and watch problem-solving videos.

Varieties of Video

Setting the goals also determines the content and "shape" of the video. For example, a popular format is the "talking head" for CEOs to convey the company's message. Alternatively, training videos use presentation slides, whiteboards, or animated content.

To decide which formats are relevant for your business, Campbell recommends reviewing the tone of your brand. Animation can convey humour, which may or may not fit your brand. However, done properly, it can also be an effective tool for simplifying complicated subjects.

Campbell has seen clients successfully use video for corporate communications as well. As he points out, an email from a business leader can be overlooked in a sea of messages. In contrast, a video message, that humanizes a leader, can be far more compelling and command more attention.

Measuring Success

As YouTube is owned by Google, the Google Analytics system is built into YouTube to gauge the success of videos in terms of viewing behaviours. YouTube has also redefined its idea of a successful video. Instead of looking simply at the number of times a video has been viewed, the new algorithm takes into account how much of the video has actually been watched, which is a more valuable measure of its engagement with viewers. If you plan to do an ongoing series of videos, viewers' comments can become a useful part of building your brand awareness, as well as a being a vehicle to collect customer feedback.

Costing Considerations

When budgeting for a video, consider the following, all of which come with a cost:

- On screen talent
- Developing and honing the script
- Location
- Lighting
- Microphones
- Teleprompters
- Post-production

Success Story

Among VMG's success stories is Vaughan Mills shopping centre. While it was well known as an outlet mall, it carried many of the same high-end brands as stores in expensive parts of Toronto. Vaughan Mills' management wanted to attract those customers, so VMG helped them create a web TV series to showcase Vaughan Mills as an experienced and upscale fashion brand. After a year, they had increased sales by almost ten percent and foot traffic by almost five percent.

BUSINESS TRUTHS ABOUT LEVERAGING THE POWER OF VIDEO

- Confirm that your target audience does indeed use videos to learn about and understand the types of products and services you offer.

- Establish a test audience to review and provide feedback on your videos.

- Budget for promoting and distributing your product/service videos.

- Plan for scenarios where videos highlighting your products, services, customers, employees or company are mocked or parodied by detractors and/or competitors.

- Focus on producing videos that are quickly viewed and easily shared.

Original BusinessCast Episode: http://bit.ly/BCPowerfulMessaging
14.37 minutes

CHAPTER 19

WHAT STEVE JOBS WOULD DO

Author Peter Sander reflects on Steve Jobs' Leadership Style

In *What Would Steve Jobs Do?*, Peter Sander distills Steve Jobs' leadership style into six "building blocks" that can be used by other business leaders. In so doing, it delves into the mind of the Apple leader to identify how his ideas and innovations brought about the success of the company. This is what makes the book different from the dozens of other tomes eulogizing the former entrepreneur, empire builder and innovator.

Sander has written over 25 books on management and brings a fresh perspective to unearthing why Jobs was able to grow a world-class company. He saw a gap in the Jobs-focused literature and wrote a book that reveals how entrepreneurs and business owners can apply the icon's unique, and often contentious, leadership style.

The Six Building Blocks

The Customer. Jobs made the effort to develop a thorough understanding of the target customer as it set the foundation for all practical innovations.

The Vision. Jobs was able to take what he knew about the targeted customer and distill it into a clear, simple vision that everyone at Apple could grasp.

The Culture. Steve Jobs disliked bureaucracy. He built a culture that served the innovation process; he made it easy for people to innovate, to want to share in solving the customer's problem and to make products they themselves wanted.

The Product. Apple's products stand out for their elegance of design, functionality, and their "cool factor". This has come about because everyone in the company strives to create products that make life better for the target customer. The company's holistic approach to solving customers' problems led, for example, to the creation of the iPod and iTunes as a means of convenient delivery that complements the original product.

The Message. Jobs evangelized Apple's products publically – demonstrating his genuine enthusiasm for each new product. This inspired Apple's employees and ultimately transformed the role of CEOs around the world from "behind the scene deal-maker" to public product evangelist.

The Personal Brand. Jobs built a reputation – both inside and outside of Apple – for creating an excellent company, an excellent work environment and excellent products. Everything he did reinforced this single-minded focus.

Many more books and movies will be written about Steve Jobs. However, Sander's work successfully captures the innovator's passion while providing practical insights.

BUSINESS TRUTHS FROM WHAT WOULD STEVE JOBS DO?

- Devote time and resources to understand your customers and their evolving needs.

- Consider holistic product development that extends beyond the creation of one product and identifies solutions that change customers' lives for the better.

- Identify the signs of bureaucracy creeping into your company's processes and culture.

- Evangelize your product by showing genuine passion for it. When you do, your target customers will be more likely to take notice and care.

Original BusinessCast Episode: http://bit.ly/BCWhatWouldSteveDo
15.28 minutes

CHAPTER 20

ACHIEVING AN EFFECTIVE BALANCE

Featuring Arlene Dickinson, CEO, Venture Communications and Founder, You Inc.

Arlene Dickinson knows what it takes to launch successful companies. She's done it herself with Venture Communications, and she's seen hundreds of others do it as a "Dragon" in the television business pitch show, The Dragons' Den. Now she's helping entrepreneurs with her most recent business, You Inc.

Dickinson describes You Inc. as a "lifestyle brand aimed at helping entrepreneurs in their personal and professional lives to grow and learn." The idea grew from the reality that entrepreneurs can't separate the business from the rest of their lives. She contends that there's not enough said about the "messiness" that emerges when personal and professional lives intersect for entrepreneurs. "This is hard," she says. "Building a business is hard work, and you're an integral part of it when you're an entrepreneur."

Achieving Balance through Advisors

At one time or another, all entrepreneurs come to realize that to succeed, they have to deal with their business lives and their personal lives. This immense pressure is frustrating, scary and lonely.

One way for entrepreneurs to achieve a workable balance between the need to be all things in their business and maintain a non-work life is to work with trusted advisors. Dickinson suggests the way to do this is to surround yourself with people who understand your industry.

An important lesson that Dickinson learned from one of her early advisors was that strong relationships with clients had to be built on mutual trust, honesty and respect. Achieving that means being transparent and continually engaging clients to ensure that you are providing them with value. Doing so builds an important "bank of goodwill".

Achieving Balance through Staff

A key method for achieving a reasonable balance is by making sure you have the right people – those who are competent, dedicated, can grow with the company, and be strong brand evangelists. Of course, it is expensive to get the right people on board; it can mean giving up equity or making concessions to entice great people to work with you. Dickinson contends, "The early days are heady and happy, with lots of activity and energy. But being able to make sure that you are building something that is sustainable takes effort." It also takes money and getting it may cost the business owner some degree of control.

It's vital for staff to feel as if they can be honest too. One of the worst situations Dickinson sees in business occurs when colleagues and/or employees hold back important information from the owner entrepreneur because they know he or she really doesn't want to hear the truth. According to her, this is the worst type of entrepreneur, one who will never grow a big, successful business.

Achieving Balance Through Clarity

All new entrepreneurs strive to do everything well – to build loyalty by serving the customer, ensure profitability and manage all aspects of the operations. To achieve the right balance, Dickinson suggests that entrepreneurs take the time to ensure that everybody in the company understands what "great" truly looks like.

She learned this herself "the hard way" in the early days of Venture Communications. Her team spent considerable time discussing and re-visiting vital details because they hadn't put a "stake in the ground" defining their values, the best way of delivering the work and the best way of handling client relationships. In short, they needed to operationalize what was acceptable and what "great" looked like for each person. Dickinson now sees that as a critical step to business and personal success.

Dickinson contends that entrepreneurs would be more successful if they take the time and energy to build a strategic framework for their brand. While they know what they want to build, they need to articulate it in ways that their people can understand and support it every day, so their client base can relate to it.

BUSINESS TRUTHS ABOUT ACHIEVING AN EFFECTIVE BALANCE

- Identify your strengths and weaknesses and surround yourself with people whose skills complement yours.

- Devote time and energy to articulate the brand (including values, personality) of the company and its products/services.

- Operationalize the brand so that people on your team know what is acceptable and exceptional.

- Draw upon trusted advisors who will provide genuine and informed feedback. If that means establishing an Advisory Board, establish a strong mandate for them.

- Let your colleagues, team, and advisors know that you value their honesty and integrity — that indeed you actually want to know the good and the not-so-good news.

Original BusinessCast Episode: http://bit.ly/BCYouInc
13.38 minutes

SECTION SUMMARY

BUSINESS TRUTHS TO SUCCEED AT EVERYTHING IN BETWEEN

BUSINESS TRUTHS ABOUT TRANSFORMING AN INDUSTRY

- Focus on establishing strong business operations while learning the industry's current rules and inherent dysfunctions.

- Secure injections of capital only when you have a strong transformational vision and strategy.

- Use your customers, analysts, and media insiders to help you identify a unique value proposition that will keep you ahead of traditional competitors.

- Focus on building your company with people who are only satisfied with making transformative change.

- Implement processes that allow you to monitor and assess business risks because introducing real transformation to an industry is accompanied by great potential as well as great risks.

BUSINESS TRUTHS ABOUT FINDING AND KEEPING THE RIGHT EMPLOYEES

- Build employee loyalty by including everyone in key organizational developments and announcements.

- Unleash the potential of people by first taking the time and effort to understand the value they can bring to the company.

- Regularly monitor Human Resources metrics that have an impact on business.

- Develop policies and processes so that people can harness social media for the satisfaction of employees and the good of the company.

- Implement an internal communications plan including tools and processes that encourage employees to feel part of a company-wide community.

- Implement a performance management program that involves everyone.

- Share with employees stories of success that strengthen the corporate culture.

BUSINESS TRUTHS ABOUT MANUFACTURING AND RETAIL DISTRIBUTION

- Manage the manufacturing and distribution of your products. If you don't have the required skills to do so, hire someone who does.

- Because protecting your brand is your responsibility, stay aware of the processes involved in manufacturing, distributing and selling your products.

- Get your products into a store where you can test its performance over time.

- Refine the packaging, the message, and the product itself until it performs well.

- Ensure your distribution partners know how and when to present your product in their promotional materials.

- Set specific goals for evaluating the effectiveness of your manufacturing, distribution and promotional partners.

BUSINESS TRUTHS ABOUT DECIDING TO RENT OR BUY YOUR BUSINESS PREMISES

- Use your business plan's projections for revenue, cash flow, human resources, client retention and I.T. to determine your needs for a business premises.

- Draw upon your team of accounting, legal, and real estate experts to develop a handful of risk/benefit scenarios for renting or purchasing a business premises.

- Reach out to the local Board of Trade or Business Association to get an overview of your community's growth.

BUSINESS TRUTHS ABOUT WORKING WITH A PR AGENCY TO TURN YOUR BRAND INTO NEWS

- When selecting a PR agency, you are largely purchasing their network of relationships with members of the media that speaks to your target audiences.

- Ask your potential PR agency to provide proof that they have indeed established relationships with members of the media that are relevant for you to leverage.

- Tie business metrics to your PR agency's activities so that you have meaningful ways for determining the value they provide.

- Allocate time to managing and monitoring your PR agency.

- To optimize your PR spend, explore those agencies that embrace package pricing or outcome pricing rather than hourly pricing.

- Research how the PR agency leverages media. The most competent agencies are adept at using today's technologies to build press for their clients

- Enable your PR agency to be effective by providing them with newsworthy stories/content. In other words, effective PR is not about distributing marketing or sales messages through media channels.

BUSINESS TRUTHS ABOUT ESTABLISHING AND SUSTAINING STRATEGIC ALLIANCES

- Before looking for a strategic alliance partner, make sure you can demonstrate that: (i) your financials are well documented; (ii) your profitability or revenue is trending upwards; (iii) your leadership team is committed to staying; (iv) you have invested in new products, new technologies or new markets; and (v) you have a clear sense of your company's core strengths and weaknesses.

- Make sure your potential alliance partner is a strategic fit, an operational fit and a cultural fit.

- "Test the waters" with a potential alliance partner. For example, conduct a time-limited and low-risk project where you can see how well you work together.

- Prior to entering any alliance, identify what success means. For example, success might be a specific number of introductions to new prospects, the amount of money saved on a joint initiative, or the total new revenues generated during a particular time period.

- Success will ultimately be defined by three goals – one that you set for your company, one your alliance partner sets for their company, and a jointly-defined goal that both of you will monitor.

- Regardless of the alliance's goals, make sure that you have the means to measure it.

BUSINESS TRUTHS ABOUT PREPARING FOR EXPONENTIAL GROWTH

- Determine whether you have the interest, skills, and mindset to lead a company that aspires to evolve beyond its current stage.

- Work with an outside consultant or Board of Advisors to help you identify the day-to-day "symptoms" of a business that is stuck in any one stage of growth.

- Work with an outside consultant or Board of Advisors to identify the skills and resources required to build systems and processes that enable the business to evolve from its current growth stage.

- Define short- and long-term goals for the company that can be tracked.

- Help people become successful by delegating responsibility and holding them accountable for their performance.

BUSINESS TRUTHS ABOUT LEVERAGING THE POWER OF VIDEO

- Confirm that your target audience does indeed use videos to learn about and understand the types of products and services you offer.

- Establish a test audience to review and provide feedback on your videos.

- Budget for promoting and distributing your product/service videos.

- Plan for scenarios where videos highlighting your products, services, customers, employees or company are mocked or parodied by detractors and/or competitors.

- Focus on producing videos that are quickly viewed and easily shared.

BUSINESS TRUTHS FROM WHAT WOULD STEVE JOBS DO?

- Devote time and resources to understand your customers and their evolving needs.

- Consider holistic product development that extends beyond the creation of one product and identifies solutions that change customers' lives for the better.

- Identify the signs of bureaucracy creeping into your company's processes and culture.

- Evangelize your product by showing genuine passion for it. When you do, your target customers will be more likely to take notice and care.

BUSINESS TRUTHS ABOUT ACHIEVING AN EFFECTIVE BALANCE

- Identify your strengths and weaknesses and surround yourself with people whose skills complement yours.

- Devote time and energy to articulate the brand (including values, personality) of the company and its products/services.

- Operationalize the brand so that people on your team know what is acceptable and exceptional.

- Draw upon trusted advisors who will provide genuine and informed feedback. If that means establishing an Advisory Board, establish a strong mandate for them.

- Let your colleagues, team, and advisors know that you value their honesty and integrity — that indeed you actually want to know the good and the not-so-good news.